JOKES for all the FAMILY

JOKES FOR ALL THE FAMILY

First published by Summersdale Publishers Ltd in 2009 as *Knock Knock: Jokes for all the Family*

This revised edition published in 2012 by Summersdale Publishers Ltd

Copyright © Summersdale Publishers Ltd, 2012

Illustrations © Shutterstock

Text contributed by Sarah Herman and Marcia Allison

Summersdale Publishers Ltd
46 West Street
Chichester
West Sussex
PO19 1RP
UK

www.summersdale.com

Printed and bound in the UK by CPI Group (UK) Ltd, Croydon, CR0 4YY

ISBN: 978-1-84953-273-0

Substantial discounts on bulk quantities of Summersdale books are available to corporations, professional associations and other organisations. For details telephone Summersdale Publishers on (+44-1243-771107), fax (+44-1243786300) or email (nicky@summersdale.com).

JOKES
for all the
FAMILY

Harry Hilton

summersdale

Contents

Funny Family

A family is like a box
of chocolates.

They're mostly sweet,
with a few nuts.

A man went to the doctor for a check-up and was told he had high blood pressure. 'It runs in the family,' he said. 'On your mother or father's side?' asked the doctor. 'Neither,' the man replied. 'It's on my wife's side.' The doctor, confused, asked, 'How can your wife's family give you high blood pressure?' The man replied, 'You try spending the weekend with them and you'll see.'

How do you make antifreeze?

Steal her pyjamas.

What's the difference between bogeys
and broccoli?

Children won't eat broccoli.

A man was in the supermarket with his baby
son who wouldn't stop screaming. As he went
around the supermarket he could be heard
saying, 'Calm down John, calm down. Don't
scream John, everything's going to be OK.'
When he reached the checkout a lady in line
gestured towards the pushchair and said,
'You're doing a great job soothing little John.'
The man replied, 'My baby's called Max.
My name's John.'

A woman carrying a baby passed the conductor as she got on the train. 'OMG!' cried the conductor, 'That is the ugliest-looking baby I think I've ever seen.' Shocked, the woman made her way to her seat and sat down. She said to the man next to her, 'The conductor was just extremely rude to me.' The man replied, 'You should go and tell the driver. I'll hold your pet monkey for you.'

A teenage girl had been chatting on the phone for about an hour before she hung up. Her father, impressed, said, 'That was a quick chat for you – you're usually on that thing for at least two hours.' His daughter smiled and said, 'Oh, it was a wrong number.'

Two four-year-old boys were overheard talking in the playground. 'My dad is a teacher. What does your daddy do?' asked the first boy. 'My daddy's a lawyer,' answered the second boy. 'Honest?' asked the first. 'No, just the normal kind,' replied the second boy.

A man is at the local swimming pool with his children, when he overhears the lifeguard shouting at his son. Turning to the boy's dad the furious lifeguard says, 'Your son was peeing in the swimming pool, and it's just not acceptable.' 'Oh, come on,' says the dad, 'all kids pee in the pool occasionally.' The lifeguard replies, 'Not from the diving board.'

Father: I think our son gets all his brains from me.

Mother: You're probably right. I still have all mine.

After staring at her granddad's wrinkly old face, a little girl asked, 'Granddad, did God make you?' 'Yes, he did – a long time ago,' replied her granddad. 'And did he make me?' 'Yes, although that was more recently,' he explained. The girl thought and then said, 'God's doing a much better job these days, isn't he?'

Teenager: Mum, can I please wear a bra?

Mum: No.

Teenager: Why? I'm nearly fifteen years old!

Mum: I won't say it again David, no!

Three naughty boys were hanging out at the zoo when the zookeeper walked over and asked them their names and what they were up to. 'My name's Joe and I'm feeding peanuts to the lions,' said the first boy. 'My name's George and I'm also feeding peanuts to the lions,' said the second. 'And what's your name?' the zookeeper said to the third boy. 'Peanuts,' he replied.

Hopping Mad

What kind of shoes do
frogs like?

Open toad sandals.

Why did the frog say 'bark'?

He was learning a foreign language.

What did the frog order at the burger bar?

French flies and a diet croak.

What's green and tough?

A frog with a machine gun.

What happened to the illegally parked frog?

He got toad away.

What did the bus driver say to the frog?
Hop on.

What's green and spins round really fast?
A frog in a blender.

What's yellow and spins round really fast?
A mouldy frog in a blender.

How do frogs die?
They Kermit suicide.

Where do toads keep their money?
In a river bank.

What's a frog's favourite lawn game?
Croak-et.

What do frogs drink?
Hot croako with marshmallows.

How did the toad die?
He simply croaked.

What goes dot-dot-croak, dot-dash-croak?
Morse toad.

Where do frogs leave their hats and coats?
In the croakroom.

What kind of pole is short and floppy?
A tadpole.

Why didn't the tadpole have any friends?
Because he was newt to the area.

What was the amphibian's job on
the cruise liner?

He was the froghorn.

What's a frog's favourite flower?

A croakus.

What's green and slimy and found
at the North Pole?

A lost frog.

SCHOOL DAYS

Why did the teacher wear
sunglasses to work?

Because his class was so bright.

After noticing a child in her class pulling faces, a primary school teacher took the troublemaker aside and said, 'When I was little my mummy told me if I pulled faces the wind would change and it would get stuck that way.' The naughty boy replied, 'Well, miss, you can't say you weren't warned.'

What do opticians and teachers have in common?

They both test pupils.

Why isn't whispering permitted in class?

Because it's not aloud.

Did you hear about the devil-worshipper who
was really bad at spelling?

He sold his soul to Santa.

Katie was late for school every day, so one
morning her teacher asked her why. 'Because
of the sign,' Katie said. 'What sign?' replied
her teacher. 'The sign that says,
"School ahead, go slow".'

Teacher: Do you have trouble
making decisions?

Pupil: Well... yes and no.

Teacher: Which two days of the week start with the letter 't'?

Pupil: Today and tomorrow.

Teacher: Who gave you that black eye, Callum?

Callum: No one gave it to me, sir. I fought really hard for it.

Pupil: Sir, my dog ate my homework.

Teacher: And where's your dog now?

Pupil: He's at the vet's – he doesn't like maths either.

A boy came home from school and told his mother he couldn't do science any more. 'Why not?' asked his mother. 'Because I blew something up,' explained her son. 'What?' she said. 'The school,' he replied.

Why did the student say his marks were 'underwater'?

Because they were below C level.

Why did the student write on his toes in class?

He was trying to think on his feet.

Why couldn't the student divide by two?

She didn't know the half of it.

A teacher was taking his first class at a new school. After introducing himself he announced: 'Stand up if you think you're stupid.' Nobody moved, and then after a minute, one pupil stood up. 'So you think you're an idiot, then?' said the teacher. 'No,' replied the pupil, 'I just didn't want you standing up all on your own.'

Did you hear about the schoolboy who put clean socks on every day?

By Friday he couldn't get his shoes on.

Why did the schoolgirl only wear one glove?

Because on the weather forecast it said it might be warm, but on the other hand it could be cooler.

What kind of exams do horses take?

Hay Levels.

Mother: Why was your exam score so low last week?

Son: Absence.

Mother: What, you missed the exam?

Son: No, but the girl who sits next to me did.

Pupil: What's the date today?

Examiner: That's not important, get on with the test.

Pupil: But sir, I want to get something right.

Child: My music teacher said my singing was out of this world.

Mum: Really?

Child: Well, she said it was 'unearthly'.

Teacher: Francis, conjugate the verb 'to walk' in the simple present tense.

Francis: I walk... um... You walk...

Teacher: Quicker please, Francis.

Francis: I jog... You jog...

In an exam room the teacher snapped at one pupil, 'Oliver, I hope I didn't just see you looking at Ella's test paper?' Oliver replied, 'I hope you didn't see me too.'

Teacher: Can anyone use the word 'fascinate' in a sentence?

Pupil: My dad bought a new shirt with nine buttons, but he's so fat he was only able to fasten eight.

Lucy: Miss, can I go to the toilet?

Teacher: Lucy, *may* I go to the toilet?

Lucy: I asked first!

A teacher arrived late to class and saw an unflattering caricature of himself on the blackboard. Turning to the class he asked, 'Who was responsible for this grossness?' Sniggering, the class joker replied, 'Well, I really can't be sure, but I blame the parents.'

A son told his father he couldn't go to school because he didn't feel very well. 'Where don't you feel very well?' his father asked. 'In school,' the boy replied.

Why did the primary school teacher marry the caretaker?

He swept her off her feet.

Teacher: How many seconds are there
in a year?

Pupil: Twelve! January the 2nd,
February the 2nd...

Pupil: I don't think I deserved zero
for this exam.

Teacher: Me neither. But I couldn't give
you any lower.

Teacher: Whenever I ask you a question, I
want you to answer altogether. What is
nine times four?

Class: Altogether!

Teacher: What is the longest word in the
English language?

Pupil: Smiles – because there's a whole mile
between the first and last letter.

Teacher: Where in England is Felixstowe?

Pupil: On the end of Felix's foot.

Teacher: What did Henry VIII do when he
came to the throne?

Pupil: He sat on it.

DOCTOR, DOCTOR

Doctor, doctor, I can't stop my hands from shaking.

Do you drink a lot?

Not really – I spill most of it!

Doctor, doctor, I keep getting pains in my eye when I drink coffee.

Have you tried taking the spoon out?

Doctor, doctor, have you got something for a bad headache?

Of course. Just take this hammer and hit yourself on the head.

Doctor, doctor, I think I'm a dog.

Why don't you sit on the sofa so we can talk about it?

But I'm not allowed on the sofa!

Doctor, doctor, I keep thinking I'm a goat.

How long have you felt like this?

Ever since I was a kid.

Doctor, doctor, there's a carrot growing
in my ear.

How did that happen?

I don't know – I planted cauliflowers.

Doctor, doctor, I keep seeing double.

Please sit on the couch.

Which one?

Doctor, doctor, my wife thinks she's a goose.

Send her in to see me.

I can't, she's flown south for the winter.

Doctor, doctor, since my operation I've had
two heartbeats.

Ah, so that's where my wristwatch went!

Doctor, doctor, you've taken out my tonsils,
my gall bladder and my appendix,
but I still feel ill.

That's quite enough out of you!

Doctor, doctor, I can't stop trembling.

I'll be with you in a couple of shakes.

Doctor, doctor, what do you charge for treating a split personality?

Fifteen pounds each.

Doctor, doctor, what do you recommend for flat feet?

Try a foot pump.

Doctor, doctor, I need something for my kidneys.

This isn't a butcher's.

Doctor, doctor, my aunt has a sore throat.

Give her this bottle of auntie-septic.

Doctor, doctor, my eyesight is getting worse.

It certainly is – this is the post office.

Doctor, doctor, my mind keeps wandering.

Don't worry – it's too weak to go very far.

Doctor, doctor, I'm just not myself.

Yes – I noticed the improvement.

Doctor, doctor, when I get up in the morning,
I'm always dizzy for half an hour.

Try getting up half an hour later.

Doctor, doctor, my sister thinks she is a lift!

Well, tell her to come in.

I can't – she doesn't stop at this floor!

Doctor, doctor, I keep seeing purple
and yellow spots.

Have you seen an optician?

No – just purple and yellow spots.

Doctor, doctor, my daughter thinks
she's an actress.

Don't worry – it's just a stage she's
going through.

Doctor, doctor, I can't stop robbing banks.

Sit down and I'll take a few notes.

Doctor, doctor, I can't stop shoplifting.

Have you taken anything for it?

Doctor, doctor, I'm only four feet tall.

You'll just have to be a little patient.

Doctor, doctor, I'm terrified of milk chocolate.

Another fruit and nut case!

Doctor, doctor, I can't get to sleep.

Sit on the edge of the bed and you'll
soon drop off.

Doctor, doctor, can I have a second opinion?

Of course, come back tomorrow.

Doctor, doctor, I can't stop telling lies.

You don't expect me to believe that, do you?

Doctor, doctor, I've got wind! Can you give me something?

Yes – here's a kite!

Doctor, doctor, I've a terrible problem. Can you help me out?

Certainly – which way did you come in?

Doctor, doctor, I've been stung by a bee. Shall I put some ointment on it?

Don't be silly – it must be miles away by now.

Doctor, doctor, my little boy has just swallowed a roll of film.

Don't panic – call me back if anything develops.

Doctor, doctor, I think I'm a telephone.

Well, take these pills and if they don't work
then give me a ring.

Doctor, doctor, I think I've been bitten
by a vampire.

Drink this glass of water.

Will it make me better?

No, but I'll be able to see if your neck leaks.

Doctor, doctor, I'm having trouble
pronouncing 'F's, 'T's and 'H's.

Well, you can't say fairer than that then.

WAGGY DOG TALES

What dog loves to take bubble baths?

A shampoodle.

What is the only kind of dog that
you can eat?

A hot dog.

What kind of dogs do vampires own as pets?

Bloodhounds.

What is a dog's favourite city?

New Yorkie.

Who is a dog's favourite comedian?

Growlcho Marx.

What do you get if you take a really
big dog out for a walk?

A Great Dane out.

What do lady dogs wear under their skirts?

Petticoats.

What did the hungry Dalmatian say
after eating?

'That hit the spots.'

Which dog needs contact lenses?

A cock-eyed spaniel.

Why is it called a 'litter' of puppies?
Because they mess up the whole house.

What kind of dog chases anything red?
A bull dog.

Why do dogs run in circles?
Because it's hard to run in squares.

What do baby dogs eat at the cinema?
Pupcorn.

How do you find your dog if he's
lost in the woods?

Put your ear to a tree and listen for the bark.

How do you keep a dog from barking in
your front garden?

Put him in your back garden.

If you take your dog into town, where
should you leave him?

In a barking lot.

Which dog can tell the time?

A watchdog.

What place of business helps dogs that
have lost their tails?

A retail store.

What did the dog do when a man-eating tiger
followed him?

Nothing. It was a man-eating tiger,
not a dog-eating one.

Why did the dog sleep on the chandelier?

He was a light sleeper.

Why are dogs so good at finding
their way around?

Because they're great at dog-raphy.

What happened to the dog that ate
nothing but garlic?

His bark was much worse than his bite.

How did the little Scottish dog feel when he
saw the Loch Ness Monster?

Terrier-fied.

FOOTBALL Funnies

Why do magicians make
great footballers?

Because they do hat-tricks.

Why don't they build football stadiums
on the moon?

Because there's no atmosphere.

What happened when the footballer
took a corner?

He turned the pitch into a triangle.

Why should you never invite a football player
to your dinner party?

Because he would spend the whole time
dribbling.

James was late for school. When his teacher asked him why James replied, 'Sorry, Miss, I was dreaming about a football match.' She looked confused and said, 'But that still doesn't explain why you're late.' He replied, 'There was extra time.'

Manager: The team's new winger cost ten million. I call him our wonder player.

Fan: Why's that? Is he really good?

Manager: No. It's because when I watch him play, I wonder why I bought him.

What's black and white and black and white and black and white?

A Newcastle fan rolling down a hill.

What's red, white and smiling?

The Sunderland fan who pushed him.

Why did the footballer take a jump rope onto the pitch with him?

Because he was the skipper.

Why did the chicken cross the football pitch?

To egg on the players.

Why did the duck get sent off the pitch?

For fowl play.

Why did the dog hate playing football?

Because he was a boxer.

Why should you never play football against a group of big cats?

They might be cheetahs.

How do you know when it's a cup draw?

The managers sit round sketching crockery.

What does the goalie like to do when he's had a bad game?

Hit the bars.

After resigning from a football club the manager gave a press conference. 'And how did the crowd react?' asked one journalist. 'Were they behind you?' The ex-manager replied, 'They were right behind me, the whole lot of them, but I managed to lose them at the motorway roundabout.'

Why don't most bankers like regular football?

They prefer fiver-side.

Schoolboy: The ref sent me off.

Mum: What for?

Schoolboy: The rest of the game.

Why didn't the sandwich show up to
football training?

Because he was only a sub.

Why will an artist never win a game
of football?

Because they keep drawing.

What did the footballer's wife say when she
went to the World Cup Final?

The world would never fit in that cup.

BEAR NAKED TEDDIES

What is a bear's favourite pasta?

Tagliateddy.

What animal cares the most about
its posture?

Yoga bear.

What should you call a bald teddy?

Fred bear.

What animal do you look like when
you're in the bath?

A little bear.

Why are polar bears cheap to keep?

They live on ice.

What's black and white and noisy?

A panda playing the drums.

What do you call a big white bear with a hole in his middle?

A polo bear!

What is a bear's favourite drink?

Koka-Koala.

Why was the little bear so spoiled?

Because its mother panda'd to him all the time.

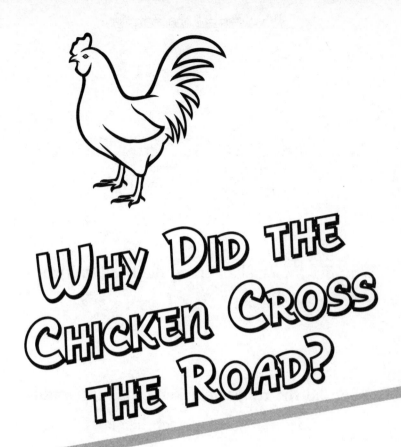

Why Did the Chicken Cross the Road?

Why did the chicken cross the road?

Don't ask us, ask the chicken!

Why did the chicken run across the road?

There was a car coming.

Why did the chicken cross the road halfway?

She wanted to lay it on the line.

Why did the rubber chicken cross the road?

She wanted to stretch her legs.

Why did the Roman chicken cross the road in a rush?

She was afraid someone would Caesar.

Why didn't the chicken skeleton
cross the road?

Because she was gutless.

Why did the chicken cross the playground?

To get to the other slide.

Why did the dirty chicken cross the road?

For some fowl purpose.

Why did the rooster cross the road?

To cock-a-doodle-doo something.

Why did the duck cross the road?
Because the chicken needed a day off.

Why did the chewing gum cross the road?
Because it was stuck to the chicken's foot.

Why did the dinosaur cross the road?
Because chickens hadn't evolved yet.

Why did the elephant cross the road?
To prove he wasn't chicken.

Why did the cow cross the road?

To get to the udder side.

Why did the fish cross the sea?

To get to the other tide.

Why didn't the skeleton cross the road?

Because he had no body to go with.

Why did the horse cross the road?

To reach his neigh-bourhood.

Why did the badger cross the road?

To visit his flat mate.

Why did the turtle cross the road?

To get to the Shell station.

Why did the dog cross the road?

To get to the barking lot.

Why did the fish cross the road?

To get to school.

Why did the chicken cross the road, roll in a muddy puddle and cross the road again?

Because she was a dirty double-crosser.

Why did the sheep cross the road?

To get to the baa-baa shop for a haircut.

Why did the donkey cross the road without looking both ways first?

Because he was an ass.

MARRY ME!

Why is marriage like a hot bath?

The longer you stay in,
the colder it gets.

A man whose house had been burgled heard that the culprit had been caught. He went straight down to the police station and demanded to speak with the burglar. The copper on duty replied, 'You'll get your chance in court, sir,' to which the man pleaded, 'Please, I just want to ask him how he got in without waking my wife. I've been trying to do that for years!'

Why shouldn't you marry for money?

You can borrow it for less.

Why is marriage like a violin?

When the sweet music's over, the strings are still attached.

On their fortieth wedding anniversary a sixty-year-old couple were granted two wishes by a fairy who appeared before them. The wife wished to see the world and 'poof', she had tickets for a world cruise. The husband wished for a wife thirty years younger than him and 'poof', he was ninety.

When a man picked his son up from school he asked him, 'What part did you get in the school play?' His son replied, 'I'm going to be playing a man who's been married for twenty years.' The father patted him on the back and said, 'Never mind, son, maybe next time you'll get a speaking part.'

Did you hear about the man who muttered a few words in a church and ended up being married?

Well, he muttered a few words in his sleep a year later and wound up divorced.

A boy asked his father, 'How much does it cost to get married?' and his father replied, 'I don't know, son, I'm still paying for it.'

A woman goes into a gun shop and asks for a rifle. 'It's for my husband,' she informs the sales assistant. 'Did he tell you what make to get?' the assistant asks. 'Of course not!' replies the woman, 'He doesn't know I'm going to shoot him.'

The bridegroom's father patted him on the back and said, 'Congratulations. Today is the happiest day of your life – enjoy it.' The man replied, 'But dad, I'm not getting married till tomorrow.' His father said, 'I know, son. I know.'

What's the difference between men and women when it comes to marriage?

Women worry about the future until they get married, and men never worry about the future until they do.

Why did Adam and Eve have such
a great marriage?

He couldn't talk about his mother's cooking.

A man is standing in front of the mirror.
He says to his wife, 'I've got a bit of a belly,
and since we've been married I've lost all
my muscle definition. And I think I might be
going bald.' His wife looks up and replies,
'Well, at least there's nothing wrong
with your eyes.'

THE BIG ROAR

How does a lion greet the other animals in the field?

Pleased to eat you.

Which animal always comes top in exams?

The cheetah.

What does the tiger say to his friends before they go out hunting for food?

Let us prey.

What did the lion say to his cubs when he taught them to hunt?

Don't walk over the road till you see the zebra crossing.

What does a lion brush his mane with?

A catacomb.

What's striped and bouncy?

A tiger on a pogo stick.

What happened to the leopard who took a
bath three times a day?

After a week he was spotless.

On which day do lions eat people?

Chewsday.

Why did the lion feel sick after
he'd eaten a priest?

Because it's hard to keep a good man down.

Knock Knock

Knock knock!
Who's there?
Old lady.
Old lady who?
I didn't know you could yodel!

Knock knock!
Who's there?
Doris.
Doris who?
Doris locked, that's why I'm knocking!

Knock knock!
Who's there?
Police.
Police who?
Police let me in, it's freezing out here!

Knock knock!
Who's there?
Luke.
Luke who?
Luke through the window and you'll see!

Knock knock!
Who's there?
Pecan.
Pecan who?
Pecan someone your own size!

Knock knock!
Who's there?
Dexter.
Dexter who?
Dexter halls with boughs of holly.

Knock knock!
Who's there?
Annie.
Annie who?
Annie thing you can do, I can do better.

Knock knock!
Who's there?
Boo.
Boo who?
Don't cry. It's only a joke.

Knock knock!
Who's there?
Lettuce.
Lettuce who?
Lettuce in and all will be revealed!

Knock knock!
Who's there?
Caesar.
Caesar who?
Caesar jolly good fellow!

Knock knock!
Who's there?
Dewey.
Dewey who?
Dewey have to keep meeting like this?

Knock knock!
Who's there?
Cherry.
Cherry who?
Cherry oh, see you later!

Knock knock!
Who's there?
Chester.
Chester who?
Chester minute, don't you recognise me?

Knock knock!
Who's there?
Don.
Don who?
Don mess about, just open the door!

Knock knock!
Who's there?
Esther.
Esther who?
Esther anything I can do for you?

Knock knock!
Who's there?
Gladys.
Gladys who?
Gladys the weekend, aren't you?

Knock knock!
Who's there?
Gopher.
Gopher who?
Gopher a long walk off a short pier!

Knock knock!
Who's there?
Hatch.
Hatch who?
Bless you!

Knock knock!
Who's there?
Who.
Who who?
Is there an owl in there?

Knock knock!
Who's there?
Nana.
Nana who?
Nana your business!

Knock knock!
Who's there?
Onya.
Onya who?
Onya marks, get set, go!

Knock, knock!
Who's there?
Ivan.
Ivan who?
Ivan infectious disease.

Knock knock!
Who's there?
Anita!
Anita who?
Anita show you something!

Knock knock!
Who's there?
Ivor.
Ivor who?
Ivor special delivery!

Knock, knock!
Who's there?
Shirley.
Shirley who?
Shirley you're tired of all these
'knock knock' jokes by now?!

Burps, Barf and Bottom Behaviour

What's brown and sits
in the forest?

Winnie's poo.

A shopkeeper greets a customer, who asks him where the toilet rolls are. 'Here you go,' says the shopkeeper. 'Did you want blue, peach, primrose yellow...?' 'White will do,' replies the man. 'I prefer to colour it myself.'

While waiting at the doctor's surgery, a man lets rip a really loud fart. Trying to look nonchalant he turns to the woman next to him as if nothing has happened. 'Do you have a copy of today's paper I could borrow?' he asks. 'No,' she replies, 'but if you put your hand out of the window you can rip some leaves off that bush.'

A famous pirate captain had a ritual that whenever battle looked imminent, he would change into his red shirt. One day his cabin boy asked him why he did this. 'It's in case I get shot,' he replied, 'I don't want my men to see the blood and get worried.' The cabin boy nodded, and then turned to see another pirate crew, sabres raised, boarding their ship. Suddenly the nervous captain said, 'Fetch me my brown trousers.'

Did you hear about the blind skunk?

He's dating a fart.

There are three ladies in a waiting room. The first lady compliments the second on her perfume and asks her what it is. 'A special blend, only available in France,' she replies haughtily. The first lady then announces that her perfume is unique, created just for her in a perfumery in Egypt. They look expectantly at the third, waiting for her contribution. She stands up and lets out a very stinky fart. 'Cauliflower curry,' she says proudly, 'from the Indian down the road.'

Why did the cantankerous old man take toilet paper to the party with him?

Because he was a party pooper.

Two flies were sitting on a dog poo. One farted and the other one turned to him and snapped, 'Do you mind? Can't you see I'm eating?'

A woman goes to see the doctor because she can't stop farting. 'It's not a huge problem because they don't smell or make a noise, but I just want them to stop. Even though you haven't noticed, I have already farted a few times in this office. Can you prescribe me something?' Looking pained, the doctor begins writing out a prescription. 'I'm prescribing some decongestants for your nose,' he says, 'and referring you for a hearing test.'

At church a little girl tells her mother she's going to be sick. Her mother tells her to do it in the bushes round the back of the church. The girl leaves and comes back after about five minutes. Her mother asks her if she threw up. 'Yes,' the girl says. 'But I didn't have to go round the back, there was a little box by the front door that said, "For the Sick".'

What do you call someone who doesn't fart in public?

A private tutor.

What did Mr Spock find in the toilet?

The captain's log.

Why do men whistle when they're sitting on the toilet?

Because it helps them remember which end they need to wipe.

Why did the baker have brown hands?

Because he kneaded a poo.

Fly Away Birdie

What's red and green and jumps
out of aeroplanes?

A parrot-trooper.

Which birds spend all their time
on their knees?

Birds of prey.

When is the best time to buy a budgie?

When they're going cheep.

Where do birds meet for coffee?

In a nest-cafe.

Which bird is always out of breath?

A puffin.

Where do parrots get their qualifications?
At a polytechnic.

What do you give a sick bird?
Tweetment.

What do owls say when it is raining?
Too wet to woo!

What kind of bird tastes fruity?
A kiwi.

Why do ducks watch the news?
For the feather forecast.

Which birds steal soap from the bath?
Robber ducks.

Where do birds invest their money?
In the stork market.

What happens when ducks fly upside down?
They quack up.

What did they call the canary that flew into the pastry dish?

Tweetie Pie.

What kind of birds do you usually find locked up?

Jailbirds.

What happened when the owl lost his voice?

He didn't give a hoot.

Seagulls fly over the sea, but what flies over the bay?

Bagels.

WICKET WISECRACKS

Why did Robin get sent off the field?

Because he broke his bat, man.

Two cricket team mates were having a pint. One said to the other, 'What's up? You're looking miserable.' The other replied, 'I am. My doctor told me I can't play cricket.' His friend looked surprised and said, 'I didn't know he was at the game on Sunday.'

What did the cricketer say when the journalist asked him to explain his poor batting average?

I'm stumped.

A batsman dismissed from the field passed the man in the white coat and snapped, 'You need glasses.' The man replied, 'So do you, mate. I'm just selling burgers.'

The Devil suggested there should be a cricket match between heaven and hell. 'That wouldn't work,' said God, smiling. 'We have all the cricketers.' The Devil replied, 'Yes, but we have all the umpires.'

Doctor, doctor, every time I use my cricket bat I feel like crying.

Perhaps it's a weeping willow.

Brian asked his boss for the afternoon off so he could go to his uncle's funeral. He actually went to a cricket match where the score was 220 for 0. Turning around he came face-to-face with his boss. 'So, I suppose this is your uncle's funeral,' said his boss, rather annoyed. 'Could be,' replied Brian. 'He's the bowler.'

The batsman collapsed in a miserable heap in the pavilion and moaned, 'I've never played that badly before. I don't know what happened.' His captain turned around and replied, 'Oh, you've played before, have you?'

Why is it called a hat-trick?

Because it's performed by a bowler.

Middlesex and Yorkshire were playing
at Lords. A man with a large white rose
approached the ticket office and asked the
price. 'Ten pounds please, sir,' was the girl's
reply. 'Well then, there's five pounds,' the man
said, handing over the money. 'There's only
one team worth watching.'

Doctor, doctor, I feel like a cricket ball.

You'll soon be over that.

Why did the American spectator cry when his team's bowler hit the stumps?

Because he thought he was aiming for the bat.

Why do most cricketers look weatherbeaten?

Because rain always stops play.

Batsman: My wife said she's going to leave me if I don't stop playing cricket.

Wicket keeper: Oh dear. That's terrible.

Batsman: Yes, I suppose I'll miss her.

FURRY FRIENDS

Which European city has the
largest rodent population?

Hamsterdam.

What are female mice better at
than male mice?

Mousework.

What kind of musical instruments
do mice play?

Mouse organs.

What has large antlers, a high voice and
wears white gloves?

Mickey Moose.

Why do mice need oiling?

Because they squeak.

What has twelve legs, three tails
and can't see?

Three blind mice.

What is small, furry and smells like bacon?

A hamster.

What are small, crisp and squeaky when
you eat them?

Mice Krispies.

What is small, furry and brilliant at fencing?

A mouseketeer.

What's the hardest part of milking a mouse?

Stopping it from falling in the bucket.

What's grey and furry on the inside and white on the outside?

A mouse sandwich.

What do mice do when they move into a new home?

Throw a mouse-warming party.

What is a mouse's favourite game?

Hide and squeak.

Who do you call if you need
a rodent-crime solved?

Miami Mice.

What do you get when you pour boiling
water down a rabbit hole?

Hot cross bunnies.

What's grey, squeaky and hangs
around in caves?

Stalagmice.

PIRATE LEG-PULLERS

What designer clothes brand do pirates love?

Arrrrrmani.

**Why do little pirates struggle
with the alphabet?**

Because they think there are seven 'C's.

Why didn't the pirate drink rum?

Because he was on the port side.

Where do pirates shop for shoes?

Clarrrrrks.

**Why can you never reach a pirate
on the phone?**

Because they leave it off the hook.

What do pirates love most about
birthday parties?

Da-balloons.

Did you hear about the pirate who got a
great deal on a new ship?

It was on sail.

What did the pirate say when it was time
for lunch?

I'm starrrrrving!

Why did the pirate make everyone bow?
Because he was being very stern.

What vegetable do pirates always eat?
Arrrrrtichokes.

Why should you never fight a pirate?
They've all got mean right hooks.

Where does a pirate keep his cows?
In his barnacle.

Where do pirates keep their valuables?

Davy Jones' Locker.

Why didn't the pirate starve on the desert island?

Because of all the sand which is there.

How do pirates pass wind?

They farrrrrt.

What did the pirate want to be when he grew up?

An arrrrrchitect.

One pirate said to another, 'That be a fine-looking hook and peg-leg ye got there.' The other replied, 'Well I should hope so – they cost me an arm and a leg!'

What has eight arms and eight legs?

Eight pirates.

What do pirates love to dance to?

Arrrrr and B.

A Man Walks Into a Bar...

A man walks into a bar with a slab of tarmac under his arm and says, 'A beer please, and one for the road.'

A man walks into a bar. The bartender chucks him out because he's too drunk. Then the drunk walks back into the bar, so the bartender ejects him again. Seconds later the drunk walks back into the bar, and just as the bartender is throwing him out of the door again the drunk slurs, 'How many bars do you own anyway?'

An Englishman, an Irishman and a Scotsman walk into a bar. The bartender says, 'What is this? Some kind of joke?'

Charles Dickens walks into a bar and asks
for a Martini. The bartender replies,
'Olive or twist?'

A neutron walks into a bar and orders a beer.
The bartender sets the beer down and says,
'For you, no charge!'

A Shetland pony walks into a bar and says,
'Can I have an orange juice, please?' The
bartender leans forward and asks, 'What was
that?' 'An orange juice,' tries the pony again.
'You'll have to speak up, sir!' exclaims the
bartender. 'I'm sorry,' says the pony, 'I'm just
a little hoarse.'

A man walks into his local and sees a tiger pulling pints. 'What are you staring at?' growls the tiger. 'Haven't you ever seen a tiger serving drinks before?' 'Sorry, it's not that,' replies the man. 'I just never thought the lions would sell this place.'

A brain goes into a bar and orders a pint of beer. The barman says, 'I'm not serving you, you're out of your skull!'

A horse trots into a bar. The bartender says, 'Cheer up, mate, why the long face?'

A pig goes into a bar and orders ten beers. When he gets up to leave the bartender says, 'Do you want me to show you where the toilets are?' The pig squeals, 'Nah, I'll go wee wee wee all the way home.'

A hot dog walks into a bar. The bartender says, 'Sorry, we don't serve food in here.'

A grasshopper hops into a bar. The bartender says, 'Wow, what an honour. What's it like having a drink named after you?' The grasshopper looks shocked and says, 'What, you've got a drink named Dave?'

A goldfish flops into a bar and looks at the bartender. The bartender asks, 'What can I get you?' The goldfish says, 'Water.'

A man walks into a pub and sits down next to a dog. The man asks the landlord, 'Does your dog bite?' 'Never!' the landlord replies. So the man reaches down to pet the dog and the dog bites him. 'I thought you said your dog doesn't bite!' the man exclaims. 'He doesn't,' the landlord retorts. 'That isn't my dog.'

William Shakespeare walks into a bar and asks for a white wine spritzer. 'I can't serve you,' says the bartender. 'You're Bard!'

What did the man say when he walked
into the bar?

Ouch!

A man walks into a bar clutching a set of
jump leads. The bartender says, 'You can
come in, just don't start anything!'

A man walks into a bar holding a pot-bellied
pig in one hand and a duck in the other. 'I'll
have a whisky,' he says to the bartender. 'And
I'll have a G and T,' says the pig. The startled
bartender gasps and says, 'Wow, that's
amazing, I've never seen a talking pig before.'
'He can't talk,' declares the man. 'The duck is
a ventriloquist.'

A man walks into a bar with a gerbil on his head. The bartender asks, 'Can I help you, sir?' 'Yeah,' the gerbil says, 'you can get this man off my bum!'

A man walks into a bar carrying a newt. 'What's his name?' asks the bartender. 'I call him Shorty,' replies the man, 'because he's my newt!'

A zebra walks into a bar and orders a beer. The bartender says, 'That'll be £5. We don't get many zebras in here, you know.' The zebra pays the bartender and replies, 'Well, at £5 a beer, I can see why!'

A man sits down at a bar and hears someone say, 'You look hot today.' A few minutes later he hears the same small voice: 'Your hair's looking great!' The man asks the bartender, 'Who said that?' 'That'll be the peanuts,' says the bartender. 'They're complimentary!'

Two bottles of probiotic yogurt walk into a bar. The bartender says to them, 'Get out, we don't serve your kind here.' 'Why not?!' screams one of the bottles. 'We're cultured individuals.'

CHRISTMAS CRACKERS

Why did the snowman call his
dog Frost?

Because Frost bites.

Two snowmen are standing in a field. One says to the other, 'Do you smell carrots?'

What do tigers sing at Christmas?

'Jungle bells, jungle bells...'

Why did the turkey cross the road?

Because he heard Christmas was cancelled over there.

How do snowmen get to work?

By icicle.

What do angry rodents send each other
for Christmas?

Cross mouse cards.

What do you call a woman with Christmas
decorations on her head?

Carol.

What do you get if you cross a tiger with
Father Christmas?

Santa Claws.

What did the pirate say when he
dressed up as Santa?

Ho, ho, ho and a bottle of rum.

What do you get if you cross a vampire
with a snowman?

Frostbite.

What did Father Christmas's wife say
during a thunderstorm?

'Come and look at the rain, dear.'

Why is Christmas like a day at work?

You do all the work and a fat man in a suit gets all the credit.

What do Christmas trees do when winter is over?

They pine a lot.

Why did the pupil do so badly in January?

Everything gets marked down after Christmas.

If you're interested in finding out more about
our humour books, follow us on Twitter:
@SummersdaleLOL

www.summersdale.com